Song of the Systole

Matthew Gagnon

SPUYTEN DUYVIL
New York City

©2017 Matthew Gagnon
ISBN 978-1-944682-70-5
Cover photograph by Aaron Siskind, Olive Tree, Corfu 33, 1967.
(c) Courtesy of the Aaron Siskind Foundation

Library of Congress Cataloging-in-Publication Data

Names: Gagnon, Matthew, author.
Title: Song of the systole / Matthew Gagnon.
Description: New York City : Spuyten Duyvil, [2017] | Includes bibliographical references.
Identifiers: LCCN 2017025930 | ISBN 9781944682705
Classification: LCC PS3607.A3586 A6 2017 | DDC 811/.6--dc23
LC record available at https://lccn.loc.gov/2017025930

For Lauralee, part of the mosaic

Contents

Solo Broadcast In Moonlight	1
Flare	3
Embryonic Fact	5
So Many Nation a Body Tries to Inhabit	6
Song of the Systole	8
Sudden Decipherment	11
Leavings	12
Detonation Point	13
The Bodies That Speak At The Helm	14
Cache	15
Song of the Neurons	17
The Tabernacle	19
Deep Focus	20
All Aboard The Sun Ship	21
Breaking News	25
Study for an Interior Dwelling	26
A Version of the Creature	27
Physique	28
Allowances After the Tradition of the Fathers	29
Song of the Cosmogonist	30
An Atmosphere of Supreme Lucidity	31
Luminous Terrene	32
Anthem	42
Simulcast	44
Flat Line	45
Song of Circumference	46
A Subject Trace	47
Some Novelties of Stagecraft	48
Evensong Treatise	50
Diurnal	51
Charter	53
I Walked With Difficulty Towards A Light	54

Study for a Sovereign Voice	55
The Spell	56
Hymned	60
Song of Drift	61
Proposition for a Structure of Urgent Care	65
Notes	67
Acknowledgments	68

We have lost.   No,
we have not lost   our way

but we have found the way

dark, hard to make out,   and yet
joyous.
                    Robert Duncan

Solo Broadcast In Moonlight

I'm filling with air.
And in me it breathes
like a broadcast
solo in moonlight.
Every bit of you
I hear, seeing inside
a protective council.
Beyond this body
you salute my ignorance.
Aloud, going lub dub
my heart flushes any
semblance of bitterness
and hears another kind
of recitation I hear
only when I stop
this titled body,
unsheathe it, let it storm.

One procession
after another.
No winding down.
Take these forceps
and extract
my beating heart.
It is hard wired
to carry fleshly accounts
and knows it must
forage now, clumsy
without its sources.
And so must burn on
a hungry thing
that digs for a kind of forest

and finds a syntax
of limits shaking
the green tones free.
The heart's composition
grows upward.
I offer tender twigs
and teach it
to burn slowly.
To gallop, as a flame
does, against
the turbulence
of convictions.

Flare

Noisy starlings own the yard.
I'm nearly worn
by proximities ripening
just out of cloud cover.
Detritus blown from wherever
scars the yard: a wind-soaked
birdseed bag, almost de-
composed cigarette butts,
lusterless wrappers
ingrained to local soil.

I know the feeling
of the world spinning.
Shit, its axis wheeled
by want and some
simple relief, to want
to waive the arrows
piercing the sky.
The world is choppy.
It's about to sink.
And if there are power lines
will they hold?

Decaying newspaper shreds
offer a soggy fragment
of partisan pledges
renewed in acidic familiarity.
My boots slosh through
deposits of sludge
and the remains
of a yard glacier
in this impermeable plot.

No thicker aversion
could unknot me
to the sensation of wading
in the saturate calm.

That's beauty for you.
Day flares on despite
my willingness to interrupt
the quiet, the wind's
shaking things up.
I am pulled closer
to this daily narcotic.
I stalk and consume
your zoned secrets
too long evaded by the clatter
of inquisitions
and molten anger.

Nervous at the feeder,
the red-bellied finch
leaves seed droppings
below for a nimble scavenger.
I flare into new values
without a nagging taxonomy.
The backyard polyphony
keens over leaf decay
and bruised wet wood.
Laureled with uncovered rot
by mid-day these wind
scattered twigs fill me empty
alive to your information.

Embryonic Fact

Understand the day is all about bearings.
It will not embody your petitions

or regard your plaint. It disassembles
your blurred vision. Set it down

as it comes, guttering with its hoarse bark.
Remember it's hard on the bones.

Follow its blusterous silence
to your yearning. A doctrine of rock

lights you up, nothing but a child
ambling into shade, what the pursuit intercepts.

Remember to swell in your grid.
The elms outside and their serrated edge.

A pursuit of clarity. How to live
within this conduct of clear edges.

So Many Nations a Body Tries to Inhabit

Surging with electrons
under a documented sun

I cleave to the meshwork
of so many questions

Through all this vision
we are falling into dusk—

a biochemical, biosphere,
compliant flame

No enchanted garden is found
in that precinct, no earthmen

but the sediment life regards
the night's primrose bloom

It is slower than salvation,
its kindling and counteractants

If a light can lead you back
into a moving picture

encircle a page where a blade is drawn
and issued intelligence

Press your thumb against
its glittering metal, a point of arrival

The page's yellow is the day
in its proclamation

The page's letters are an industry
of refusals, they are older

than a cipher spelled
by a hand on a page

Song of the Systole

Aye, 26 letters installed
on my tongue
gyrate like a weeping turbine.
A little black box
records each irregularity,
fusing the green
intimacy of the day
with the air's disquiet.
I could list the colonies
we happen upon,
a commonwealth of hands
reshaped to each
enjoinment—eye to render
ear to vicinage,
body to disremember.

*

I remember we formed
difficult words: cleave,
forthwith, diurnal, contraction.
Resemblances, if not
approximate models.
Arise with the crimson sky,
newly fallen in a curve of light.
This is a day of deadlock,
though this is not conclusive.
I will not set the house on fire
or find us between a seam
where your fingers
wander certain edges.
Did I say this was literal,
conclusive, anechoic?

*

The day is not formless.
I am a braided body
a child overflowing with oxygen.
This is a day I am singing
from your body,
have the right of way
in my weaving.
Our mouths touch
at an estuary's lip.
Such things as degrees.
Anything overheard
translated by the row of trees
how their roots clamor
and sip the water
of our ways, our bodies
a locus of giving.

*

I do not remember saying
the streets were strewn
with bodies discovering
their imperfect girth,
persona of things fixed
in the margin.
I do not remember
dreams filled with boreal
climates, oracles,
the complete stutter
of closure, a fieldbook
for edible parts.

*

I sing as if read
in that place of torn things
unspared as the hours
stagger, my hands levy
the commerce
of sudden departures.
You rive matter,
watch it yield a covenant.
Not out of obligation,
but a theory of hydraulics
pushing a basket
of undecipherable glyphs
down the falls.
Any geologic fault
would bracket
this aorta, allow
the ciphering
to swell in the draft.

*

This is a day we remember
for its dispossession.
This is the day
we left something out.
A beginning
or ending, a quantity
of beginning
or ending, a whole world
taken back.

Sudden Decipherment

A smokestack is the value
of knowing

precisely where you are mapped

but this rent heart
is tuned to capsize

in sudden decipherment

The grass is swaying toward
a theology

ticking toward a body bruised
with begetting

unloaded into a system

The chronometer is right
reorient yourself

Leavings

What's unbridgeable as you step inside the pantheon, city of memorials? We observed a petrograph from a buried atmosphere, as if behind glass the world throttled our windpipes with homesickness. To be hedged by a possession, an object once loved. I am transpierced with a desire for a sign beyond the periphery. Describe the last appendage to be cut, replaced by a prosthetic heart. An alluvial plain opens with its leavings: ice age, rock age, a calculated deed.

Detonation Point

Say this isn't why
we detonate.

We molt out of a habit,
its ideas that wash us
blank, back into a variable.

I brace for the dust
cloud, an ocean
that goes uninjured,

an ocean I stand beside,
shoreless, an ocean that cannot
say 'aglow' behind my eyes.

The Bodies That Speak At the Helm

Stay inside the one enduring thing
cathartic in currency

Every phrase is a chapel
a frayed tanglement

unsealed into its belonging

I could offer a topology of inscriptions
that pierce a habitat

a thrum of small collisions

The fingertips welcome, graze, trespass
the abdomen's grammar

besiege a written complex
of apprehensions

we speak as one body at the helm

Cache

Things expand and contract.

Complete in their intercellular roughage
I diagram their name:

a blush for reticence, a mouth
that opens with an O
to cross-examine a tumescent smile,

a cache of failure in rigor.

I've been listening
to your breath expand,

its ferine potentiality
infixing a forbidden
autarchy.

In the day's afterlife

I thrash against the alluvium
of hesitancy.

Its mechanics can
say anything, capsize
into a siege of suggestion.

What looks like the curvature of a face
offers its ambient equipoise,

partitions and bowed shape
we go between.

All the way to these
haunted dormitories,
never disclose your name.

I am startled to your beacon:

buoyant in the dusky
nothing of unmooring
in this quiet wreck.

Song of the Neurons

Sing in me oneironaut
lug me aboard your stretch

of bursting capillaries, your ozone's flex

My heart is made of graphite
it is your continent, your sprawl

*

There are tendons in this system
that archive laughter, a sonic fabric

that torches air, an inchoate profusion

of arrivals and flight risks
uncontained in the day spray's

gleaming translucent blooms

*

I am transported back into a boy

yawning into charred driftwood
caught on the lip of a shore

I have met my gladiators in the distant
speck of a darker shade of want

their homespun ethic scores a name

cast of a face remembered
its glow, and transcription-like afterimage

*

Everything here is spatial, spatially kept

Overcome home, be overcome
the sparrows fill the airwaves

Embrace this, what the matins meant
it's not strategic, reluctance I don't know

*

Welcome to the homing frontier

Nothing but a species of quiet and sung data
in an early hour binocular watch

Does this fathomage construe return?

Do the synapses tell a body apart?

The Tabernacle

But it is nothing
that stands against the welter of impact

dog-eared with dusk   a projection
of dusk

its lack of light reported on tile
finds a foundation

its violence
perfectly contained
closes there

in the body
pierced by coherence—

its archways and aqueducts   sunken charts
and basins of overflowing light

that shelters nobody
no body
as sown to its den

Deep Focus

With mouth agape over a leaden field
you listen for a name, a sun, a moon overhead.

If fire, if breath burns a language without continuum
something illegible drifts into a cry.

A fire briefly blooms. Unspools.

In this roiling dust, breath is sucked
into a throat's tap until it scars.

Dry leafage. Tinder. Wind thrown.

The near begins as a line of sight
protracting, projecting.

Here is nearness in the migratory pitch and whine
the warble and strain in the throat.

Under a sun shot shroud, you blur into
a blazing, protein sky.

Set the land straight and good.

Set the millstone down.

All Aboard the Sun Ship

1

Alack, the day. Are you
still here among the indices?

There's a rallying point,
the crescendo of voices

brought to the chopping block.
You might say no rationale declines

an overture of overlapping slate
baking in dry heat, or detest

that a lack of water brings dust
before the day is done.

We are buried in errata, communiqués,
a border's altissimo cry.

This terra parches wonderment
and leaves us still and ghosted.

Pages pried from the loom.
Omitted footprints in the sand.

2

It's a dent in the metal that wakes us.
An issued sound that we say is not the cry

of emancipation, not a bodement nearing hiatus.
A figure is fragmented, drawn into ceremony.

The painter on the roof overlooks
the sheen of a sun drenched valley,

how things appear as they are, stitched
with light, shocked into sight.

He chooses to invent a man from cobalt blue
upon his blind return to the streets.

Nearby there is a table outside a café
where two people have talked, a word of war

turns to a blemish, a word of need.
And we are here in the swarm

of circumstance, in the rickety dome
suckling our sallow focus.

3

Speak loudly in your mother tongue,
the letters make lips dry

and cracked with compunction.
A wind blows through a cypress

where your voice becomes
a garden of withering azalea.

On this day, the dead
are an alter of marigolds.

On this day, the marksman's eye
is accurate and obedient.

It knows the prime of sight
locks into a warm-blooded source

unthreading the air with fatigue.
Speak loudly, the sparrows

are calling to the apogee
in the solar day.

4

Buried in errata, regalia, salute,
we didn't remember

the conversions of a windmill
securing a savage wind.

Asked about the earthenware globe
that cracked under our thunder,

we said a map is a cluster of forms,
burnt interiors immersed

in remembered vistas.
Like clockwork, cartilage tears

in the regiment's primitive slash,
a watchword making fast.

As the dust migrates and follows
the path of least resistance

we sleep on a bed of anemone,
our words thrown down on slate.

Breaking News

Amid a conflicting report
a nuthatch fetches a black fly,
dips its plume in a stagnant pool.
This is a sky drawn, grafted,
rescued, not a bath of vapors an afternoon
shutters with counterfeit meaning.
It is just an incident within
a field of possibility, something periodic
and bruised, one location
in which we grip that instant of contact.
Upstream a scarecrow is ragged
in the wounding, a music of terror
barely rises above the slopes,
reft with nothing
but its melody's radius,
the slow ancient call of the bird
in the distant flicker.

Study for an Interior Dwelling

If revolt were material
a cosmology is what we subtract.

The atoms are inflamed
in a bedimmed resistance.

Remember the interior shine
is all racket and commotion

it's where you go, steady now
with a nerved blast.

Make dark the rhetoric
its molecular advance
twilit, sheened, abraded.

A Version of the Creature

It is difficult to hear
in these rooms,
our version of want.
What windows flaunt
on greasy panes
won't intervene
with the still cool stubble
of newly cut grass.
Domestic chatter
arches over doorways
at cross-purposes:
old wood absorbs us.
Floorboards grant
frantic footfall.
Hides thicken. Adrift
through morning thaw,
we rejoin to a parted
curtain. A crow's throaty
alert stalls us slack,
then sheathes its starched
call, no trace left.

Physique

Against an abridgement of light
you dispatch an outline.
This is a reading room
lettered and jeweled with happiness.
Only a complete silhouette
troubled by the tone of wanting
more than an aisle,
more than a coordinate of survival.
Among the winter scarves
no frozen constitution
keeps time along the metronome,
how we startle awake,
generous through the transpositions of our ark.
This is a reading room
I've chiseled back
from an uncertain luminescence.
The purpose of a torso
wires relief and offers
revival to my amen.

Allowances After the Tradition of the Fathers

An igneous thing in the hard light

I begin in distances, branched and nervy
down to this single file stumble

Let there be a crude blue sea, aflame
and in back of me

Only the light figures here

Only the light leaves a touch sensitive muscle
for memory, for broadening ripplets

Let there be a muscle to describe
the gauzy recalcitrant dark

More sentience hidden in the wood

Leaves burn in the mouth of the house
this property burning, opening

a ghost lit between interior beams

Let there be an image for labor
for time, for anger

Song of the Cosmogonist

It's not the proof
but the passage
holding you skyward

when all the underwood
is beginning to rot.

Looking glass blue,
every captive bray
is translated from you.

The booming intonation
of hymn, hallo, hello

throbs in its panic
with all the leaf stammer.

When the dilating globe
is an anthem of you

it fetches the heady
boom of liberty
like a final discourse.

An Atmosphere of Supreme Lucidity

The heat here is unparalleled
barely discernible.
When heat rises we're stroked
into a dark watercolor
angled to defeat.
Such a surface pressure
sketched into a limitation.
A song perhaps gently flawed
represents a populace.
What is tender, unhurried.
Recover a ravished ground
as though pierced
with arrow, bullet, alarm.
Only the signs of collateral
damage, the thaw of counterparts.
I'm holding the last fiber
in a sprig of novocain.

Luminous Terrene

"Around me now, at sunset, the flood of people walking by swelled and then subsided, their voices and languages passed through me as though I were made of glass."
       Emmanuel Hocquard

A gyre of minerals is visible from the outcrop, but can we really say we'd rally behind the visible?

I won't be extracted from a custom or assembled into the fold of a wave.

A flock of fish is breathing on dry land. There's nothing modern about the way we cook fish.

An aggregate of water over a film of water. Do we tread the water's timetable, survey the riptide's antinomy?

Read the night as if the night is read, and in stoking the night, order it: punctuated.

Fastened to the umbrage of what's missing, my memory's adrift in a receding tidemark.

***

History replayed again and again, a narrator the last sizzling thread of smoke in an ashtray.

Despite the patter of feet edging along the subplot, you're reinvented in close-up.

Is it possible to love more than one world, to see clear across to the other side? Can a void be touched?

For all the stash of mechanics I hold like a baby over my heart, I'm bound in bindweed, held like a breath on a frontier.

This production of matter is dispatched into a form of recognition. Something habitable.

You're superimposed against a disestablished agency.

***

Here's an independent archeology, a cuckoo's call tongue-lashed, ridden with peril.

A scandal of signage follows. The body's many tributaries transferable in forfeited climate.

Trailing the mottled geography of the mouth, a smudge of ink is in flower.

To be rewritten with an engine's upkeep. Idling engine of a saga or fable exposed to a voice camouflaged in a thicket.

That's the postscript. Part sediment, part siren, part fluttering eyelid betraying the precision of its gaze.

A tracking shot catches the precise angle when light is suddenly caught, exuberant with dust.

***

A voice undresses on the screen; it crackles toward a lost gravity, navigating a sinking argosy.

Given the market equation is precisely what you think, you might ask where the replicas fit in, if anything's trainable, digits over water.

Asleep inside the mirror, you vanish inside of it by day's end.

You're weightless, perhaps disembodied, billowing in the draft.

You unfold into the solitude of an hour's climate, incarnating a tentative law.

There's a prefigured breeze in the plenum, an assembly of static matter engineering a phoneme.

***

I said rain is not a marker or an afterthought. Then I said rain spills from the air connected to a cable.

The flight pattern is finally stabilizing. We're crisscrossing our way through a field of dense particulates.

We seek pleasure in learning how to tremble, but a language is abandoned rather than absorbed.

Will the blowdown leave us shelterless and exposed? Is it laying the lozenge of grief on our tongues?

There's the psalmist singing from the gully. Things enkindle slowly.

An aspen leaf quivers in the rain, a ready alibi flanked by smoky light, and shaken from the branch.

***

It isn't the full-fledged rumor, but the flames burning the building in which you disappear.

Does any transaction involving legal tender leave a trail of condensation that cuts across time? Can we tenderize the money into love?

Say anything but your room is foreclosed: take the courtyard covered in moss.

I've blinked my way through a concentration of vaults, given exurbia a taste of honey.

We are discovering theories of interference as a throng of headlights jams the sector.

In contrast to an examiner of ancient parchment, you inch your way into apprehensions of emergency.

**

You could be anyone or anything: a wave of voltage passing through a body, thistles in lumen passing through a body.

Is a complex field of visual data, like a bare-boned tree or a stand of lichen interrogating a stone, closer to an erotic?

At this moment in time information is passing through a body.

Neither a clump of displaced earth or a pirouetting wind is recognized for being a sign of ruin.

Are the mechanisms of governance indelible? Shall we listen from our mounds of labor, unquestioned by immaculate refuge?

This wealth of transmissions sounds like a sob, an outer frequency unarmored and splicing the dark matter.

***

How does one handle the circumference of a lamp in whatever uncertain position its light progresses?

The rift was a form of grievance, not a dynasty throwing its halo on a page.

Across a hearthstone, a shadow is searching for a body.

This was the contour of a ghost without any material presence, without any architectural trace.

It was as if we were being thrown into relief, searching for a new vessel.

My desire became a territory, a beacon in a forest of shipwrecks.

***

To come to rest at a clearing, let's not be warned there's a map buried under the guise of extinguishment.

The wheeling trade winds hold nothing back. They can't rescue you or be the untroubled agent passing through.

As a storm forms on the shuddering frame of a proposition, a terminus forms.

A tidy domestic sweep worries the nest. I'm arrested in a final meteorological reading.

It's a cadence inside the scroll, a radiant threshold I daub with the seduction of reenactment.

The flagging moon is part of a visual syntax, another system that molds a hemisphere, a tidal force that doesn't pine for a doctrine of discontinuity.

***

There's a landmark and a probable cause exfoliating into a contested territory.

This native place administers suspicion, circulates a remedial panic.

A shadow knows its countenance is just becoming, heart valves thrumming.

You could be a veil, voice, or frame, gaining entry into the atmosphere, a disturbance depicted and apprehended.

Could the gap between radical bewilderment and the specter of renewal, bring us closer to a clearing where the ambit of the possible might bloom us into an intoxicant?

This could be a film. A film we've seen before. A film we're watching as it tells us this is where the light exits.

Anthem

If I'm not tuning out
then I'm tuning in.
You might say I'm up against
a fractured anthem.
The warped frame
of a picture we're leaving
replays in an endless loop.
We're not obliged
to return to this.

A singular imprecision
leafing through a mechanism,
tied to anything you say
as sound to sound.
Your faint shudder against
the slurred perspective
has little to do with applying
pressure to a linguistic sign,
and more to do with how
you put an accent on what's
being preserved in amber,
the groove of a disk.

We're in need of a fix
when the tarmac buckles
under a hangover.
A sundial dismounts.
The mapping is not a territory
but a reserve deposit
processing shades of grief.
Once, in an indentation
of sky, the lighting fell
out of reprieve.

For once, a situation
needs a scene to set the stage.
The décor's in chrysalis
gilded in lacy stuff.
In every affect there's
a doctrine. I can see its frayed
shadow emerging in radar.
It radiates under any measure
of light without a compass.

Eventual mention or woe.
The chemistry between us
calls us out of the grid,
landlocked in some
superimposed plexus.
Even the fault lines of a revolution
finally fall into the wealth
of an assignment.
Neither a doorjamb
or doohickey. Yet
there are unwound spools of film
left in substantial neglect
flawless in what they deal.

Simulcast

Into the bare fact of our station, we're holding a greased needle up to the light. The speech is degenerative. When we were gardening through the texts our images relied on, we unearthed a medical kit, learned how to drape the alphabet from a relay device. Auctioned for a set price, the inflation rate is adaptable. The remedy dissolves leaving a burn mark. Left to decipher a taxonomist's poverty, we felt as if painted onto a globe viewed from space, hanging fragile, serpentine. An image of ambience floating, nationless. The divine inside the barrel of a needle. Up to the light. If our wounds are pressed against wordlessness, are they hotly contested junctures protruding from a blown circuit? The primordial emits a sound barely heard through the speaker. From the cut, we say formative and plastic is our speech, a voluntarily derived coat of sound we pull from a tube. We resist our own labor.

Flat Line

Pleated with logo
this is the music
calibrated to a crude decibel.
I'm slowly embroidered
into an ontology.
Every day ambush.
Every day a hierarchy of need.
There is the maypole
keeping the vital signs
fathomless in gauze.
There is the radar
scanning for a flat line
in a speck of sky.
Once the sun shower stopped.
Its river melted
in what I thought
was a forgery.

Song of Circumference

Around a periphery
a world insists a world

to carry a lived refrain

Dimly lit, dimly given
some gleaming returns

Cleared from collapse
our nests endure

such extremities

Reach within, feeling there
for becoming motion

Our faith in all
circumferences

A Subject Trace

He awaits the breaking
news of the nuclei   flaking outward

absorbed onto a surface
of inducement

He is at once a subject   whipsawed
with a greater efficiency

From his commission
recanted in microtone

the moist earth is unafraid
of brutality

arid static   channels of devotion

Some Novelties of Stagecraft

We are distinguished once our punch line is underwritten.

It's the sound of a river churning, assertive in its nothingness.

Water threads everywhere, making the world wetter, making the debris float, an unchosen act expanding.

Life here is phantasmal. Globed, then photographed, blurred on the edge of what?

At first, we said like night and day, the poles are in the pipeline.

The survey began an unfiltered instrument, compressed like a pearl, sunk in a moment's precise formation.

Explain how we amass a gabled domain, how we annotate this dynamo axing through the sylvan shade.

In a veneer of playing roles, I'm storied and customized, a shimmering monument blowing things into revolt.

To say it softly, as in the morning quiet, I'm packing heat. That fuse box is humming beside a thornbush.

If there's enough irrational exuberance to tie us both to the tracks, does our body become a swooning emissary, a lock of nightfall unsnarled?

Instantly on special terms with a tropical wind, we could make this mourning a payload, a meteor of easement.

Unfurling my flag cloaked with a centennial's disquiet, I'm programming in deference to a stagecraft embalmed.

A plot strategy or error of judgment, we say our lives are swaddled by small recognitions.

Evensong Treatise

It's not the first time
we're being bombarded
by a lack of direction.
All manner of speaking
recognized as artifice
cleanly subtracting what we see.
These fragments to which
we adhere some stitch.
Look for the rootstalks
advancing us through the static
guiding us through
the rhetoric of birdlime.
If clinking on brick or glass
edges us closer to a harmonic
we dare not trespass
or come apart unwoven.
Look to the furnishings
timbered into a voice
something like observance
is netting a soapbox.
There's the dead weight
dark as a lodestar.

Diurnal

1

Built to spell the tether
and junctures
the forecast has its turf

It is the day's aggrieved motto
a cask of bearings

A word: envoy   port   call

would rather reverberate
among the stones and minerals

than wither to zero

2

It is the clemency
of the present
in the footlights that imperils

Navigate the boulevards edged with wire
and columns of solar glare

There is no terrace of purveyance
that counts the losses
how they stick like an outgrowth

letting those subatomic particles re-
assemble an eye's globe

as a voice learns reluctance

Charter

Everything's reared to dissuade rain.
Thus water tracks into a house.

Such ligatures of pathologic query
burn in a beautiful machine's refuge,

a scrawling in the human fat,
sheathed in an extremity of ground.

What we want to pronounce
but cannot say: figment, remnant, remember.

Palms are laid down in dim corridors.
At dusk the lights are heavy in their blinding.

Flesh emerges from liquid,
lurks behind a charter of salt.

What we hold down and serve,
bodies revised by a dusty atrium.

We lift the hammer to strike
the letters left on an anvil.

An implacable alphabet now granulated
covers a network of nerves.

It swells like a hive without
withholding our light.

A warm provision of letters
splices our infrastructure.

I Walked With Difficulty Towards A Light

Though the light lands in grey misted
ambience   the light on the wharf

on the ropes holding the ships
their inheritance   the footfall
on wooden planks   voices catching wind

though the light disperses them
stretches across the harbor

in mist   in dissipating intelligence

A clarifying mist   a myth
of place where I walked
with difficulty towards a light

towards the anchored boats   shimmering
small animals unsure

A habitat holds things open
to a breathing potential

where I go   to toll with liberty
to float in its going

Study For A Sovereign Voice

The man was not an architect, he did not spin
the wheel of hazard to a revolution,
imagining the torn sinew a probable cause.

A sleeper on a bed of cartridges, he excavates
the myth of driftwood, scribbles notes
at a site he had thought rapidly dissolving.

There is grief he said, there is something
my eyes could not have seen as a theorem.
His name is an unanswered question.

Twined to a cosmology of herbs and ink,
he did not model bayonets out of clay
or wet the vault of the hollow conch shell.

With white powder stained on his
fingertips, he drew a letter inside a cave
both forgotten and not forgotten.

He was not seen through the gunsmoke,
through the portent of a clearing.
His sovereign voice is an avalanche of bees.

The Spell

1

It is the spells they make
an eye gathers

its threaded knowing

torn from a warm
evening's pledge.

This is a perimeter, an echo flowering.

This is a day's undoing
its speed and slack

of giving

as a body falls entire
into invisibility.

2

From threshold
to threshold

it is given and pledged.

If the body lacks
any economy of giving

if the body's fibers unravel.

In a field of witness
does it ripen back to a distillate?

A body is scrolled in laurel

scrolled with forgetting
and departure.

3

Is it the spells they make?

This is a sector
where several bodies meet

at the omission of a margin.

This is a habitat of briar
a flexuous source

in a refuge of inquiry and withdrawal.

A lexicon wavers.
Even adrift

panic is a form of intimacy.

They stroke and polish
the hourglass

near gone, nearly given.

4

If a spell is unspoken

this will be a body, my body
moved and startled with clarifyings.

These surfaces distort a field, don't they?

Now that they open
yielding information—

touch recognition.

No eve of abandon
or horizon of wavelengths

but the individuated pulse.

A bouquet of mouths
bloom there

in pledge and giving.

Hymned

Something comes forth

Hymned into being

this flesh is not your permanent
household

held like a brittle stick

held to you distantly

I become that taut figure
warming to take good care

to be hymned and quartered

on the threshing floor

If leaf, if green
was the air

Song of Drift

There was drift
and the rasp
of a nightingale

singing and unstringing
an open wound.

It is the insinuation
of a furnace blast

that shudders things
near to a lisp
a burr caught at the base

of the throat.

*

Loosened from a cast,
I've patiently waited
to keep vigil over the returning
and belonging, the murmur
of the drowning man.

A cantillation begins
in the abdomen.

Permission has its depths
rather than eclipsing
the hierophantic tongue.

*

I am eased into a horizon
of soluble psalms
with which I unmake a poem,

lashed by breath
and offering an exegesis
of conquest,

the unveiled
and delinquent story

told in a lock of hair.

It's not too late
to be unearthed.

*

Arteries fill with knots of light,
particles of sound
deviate from their course
spending another void
with that ancient risk—
the heart readily tries us.

A savant is sitting in his garden
losing the intervals
he has taken for a purity of place.

Every trajectory the body
gives to describe its property
becomes a sundered failing

turning its mind to the expression
of coalescence, a book
fallen from deep space
filled with enigma.

    *

False starts are inevitable.
False notes in a chemical reaction.

Every breath is an exfoliator
with its vocalized fable
testing the logic of aerodynamics,
studying the tendencies
to drift into something permeable.

Something isolate
as it makes a counterpoint
in its undoing.

    *

If I am a mortal orbit
gathering my share
of marrow and density.

If I become lost in the rows
of data extending
to no living thing,

birthing a prototype
of a mourned inquest.

If I withdraw inside
my carapace, it is with an orphan's
yearning to anoint
the eroding body

with a craving for the ways
of the occupying beyond.

Proposition For a Structure of Urgent Care

Should I take this poem
to bristle, to go bullish

into the courtyard, or to say
the poem is kinetic and it

moves without stridency
with the force of a supplication?

I take my chances to grieve,
to be hounded by rituals of loss.

It's hope, like a lathe,
deforming the newsfeed.

The acknowledged ambition
to smuggle your visage, baby,

into the poem, to duel
what otherwise erodes this heart,

that howling, world.
Who wouldn't petition

the flesh, a nutrient overcome
with transferals?

Fill my lot with the unanswerable.
Something canny

drawn from madness.
What if the poem was a hearth

and I offered you, in real time
the accrual of joy.

The song can shoulder
this urgent care.

A vital syntax subtracted
from the total.

Notes

Deep Focus is a photographic or cinematographic method offering a rich depth of field where the near and far receive equal weight of focus.

"An atmosphere of supreme lucidity" is a line from Frank O'Hara's poem, "In Memory Of My Feelings."

"I walked with difficulty towards a light" is a line from Alexander Sokurov's film, "Elegy of a Voyage."

Acknowledgements

My gratitude goes out to the editors of the following journals in which the poems in this book, sometimes in earlier forms, first appeared: *The Nation, Hambone, WebConjunctions, Colorado Review, Boston Review, LVNG, 1913: A Journal of Forms, American Letters & Commentary, Fourteen Hills, The Laurel Review, Model Homes, Phoebe, Sentence: A Journal of Prose Poetics,* and *Upstairs At Duroc (France)*.

Thanks to Nathaniel Mackey and Michael Boughn for selecting the poems "Allowances After the Tradition of the Fathers" and "Flare" for *Resist Much/Obey Little: Inaugural Poems to the Resistance* (Dispatches Editions/Spuyten Duyvil Press, 2017).

Many thanks to Lewis Freedman and Lesley Yalen of Agnes Fox Press for printing "Luminous Terrene" as a chapbook in early 2013.

Grateful acknowledgment to the Aaron Siskind Foundation for reproduction permission.

Special thanks to Peter Gizzi, Bradford Morrow, Patrick Pritchett, Andrew Mossin, Matt Hanson, Carl Kelleher, Nicholas Rattner, and my parents, Michael and Lynda.

Sincere thanks to Tod Thilleman for taking on *Song of the Systole* and letting it meet a reader's generosity.

And most of all, thank you to my wife, Lauralee, who plays a vital role in this endeavor and who listens to the words as they come.

MATTHEW GAGNON teaches writing at Westfield State University and the University of Connecticut, Hartford. He is a graduate of the MFA Program for Poets & Writers at the University of Massachusetts, Amherst. His poems have appeared in many journals and magazines, including *1913: A Journal Of Forms, American Letters & Commentary, Boston Review, Colorado Review, Denver Quarterly, Fourteen Hills, Hambone, LVNG, The Nation, WebConjunctions*, and in the anthology, *Resist Much/Obey Little: Inaugural Poems To the Resistance* (Dispatches Editions/Spuyten Duyvil Press, 2017). He lives in Easthampton, Massachusetts, with his wife and daughter. *Song of the Systole* is his first full-length book.

www.ingramcontent.com/pod-product-compliance
Lightning Source LLC
Chambersburg PA
CBHW021158080526
44588CB00008B/394